A GLASS OF BITTER

A PLAY IN ONE ACT

by

J. B. PRIESTLEY

SAMUEL · FRENCH

LONDON
NEW YORK TORONTO SYDNEY HOLLYWOOD

Copyright © 1954 by J.B. Priestley
All Rights Reserved

A GLASS OF BITTER is fully protected under the copyright laws of the British Commonwealth, including Canada, the United States of America, and all other countries of the Copyright Union. All rights, including professional and amateur stage productions, recitation, lecturing, public reading, motion picture, radio broadcasting, television and the rights of translation into foreign languages are strictly reserved.

ISBN 978-0-573-02083-4

www.samuelfrench.co.uk
www.samuelfrench.com

For Amateur Production Enquiries

United Kingdom and World excluding North America

plays@samuelfrench.co.uk
020 7255 4302/01

Each title is subject to availability from Samuel French, depending upon country of performance.

CAUTION: Professional and amateur producers are hereby warned that *A GLASS OF BITTER* is subject to a licensing fee. Publication of this play does not imply availability for performance. Both amateurs and professionals considering a production are strongly advised to apply to the appropriate agent before starting rehearsals, advertising, or booking a theatre. A licensing fee must be paid whether the title is presented for charity or gain and whether or not admission is charged.

The Professional Rights in this play are controlled by United Agents LLP, 12-26 Lexington Street, London W1F 0LE.

No one shall make any changes in this title for the purpose of production. No part of this book may be reproduced, stored in a retrieval system, or transmitted in any form, by any means, now known or yet to be invented, including mechanical, electronic, photocopying, recording, videotaping, or otherwise, without the prior written permission of the publisher. No one shall upload this title, or part of this title, to any social media websites.

The right of J.B. Priestley to be identified as author of this work has been asserted in accordance with Section 77 of the Copyright, Designs and Patents Act 1988.

CHARACTERS

Norah Grant
Fred Grant
Evie Pell
Detective Inspector Hammond
Roy

The scene is the sitting-room of the Grants' house in a North London suburb

Time—the present

INSPECTOR HAMMOND

Scene is the sitting-room of the Grants' house in a North London suburb

Time—the present

A GLASS OF BITTER

SCENE—*The sitting-room of the Grants' semi-detached villa in a North London suburb. About nine o'clock on an autumn evening.*

It is a comfortably furnished room of an ordinary kind. There is a door in the R *wall leading to the front door and one in the* L *wall leading to the kitchen and the back of the house. There are windows—not high, but the small, low type—in both the* L *and* R *walls. The essential furniture is a small table* C *with an easy chair either side of it; two or three extra chairs and one or two other pieces of furniture as available can be used to dress the stage. The piece can be played without a proper set, merely suggesting the doors and windows and using only the essential furniture.*

(*See the Ground Plan at the end of the play*)

When the CURTAIN *rises* FRED *and* NORAH GRANT *are sitting each side of the table* C, FRED *in the easy chair* R *and* NORAH *in the easy chair* L. *He is reading an evening paper, pipe in mouth.* NORAH *is doing some mending. It is a very quiet, dull, domestic scene, typical of millions. Fred is a man about fifty, pleasant enough but rather formidable, a man who could lose his temper. It is plain he is devoted to his wife. Norah is some years younger, in her middle forties, fairly attractive in a soft, humdrum sort of way. She is equally devoted to her husband but a little afraid of him—he is the boss.* FRED *reads and* NORAH *goes on with her mending for about half a minute or so after the* CURTAIN *rises. Then he puts the paper on his knees and she, looking across, catches his eye, and they smile.*

FRED (*without rising*) I think I'll walk down to the Lion and have a glass of bitter . . .
NORAH (*smiling*) Yes, why don't you, Fred?
FRED. Only one, mind you . . .
NORAH. I know . . .

FRED. But I'll linger over it. They certainly don't make much out of me at the *Lion*—still, they always seem very pleased to see me.

NORAH. That's because they know you're a very nice man.

FRED. I hope so. But what they don't know—is that I've got a wife who's better still—one in a thousand . . .

NORAH. Who'd rather stay at home—and finish her mending . . .

FRED. Now you're sure about that?

NORAH (*smiling*) You know I am. So long as we have our night out at the theatre fairly often, I'm satisfied. But you stop that and you *will* get into trouble, Fred Grant.

FRED (*rising*) Wouldn't dream of it. (*He looks round contentedly and then looks at her*) We haven't done badly, have we? For two people who married rather late, didn't have children, we've made a good job of it, if you ask me. Neither of us was the easy marrying kind—you were too reserved, too particular . . .

NORAH (*not annoyed; still smiling*) All right, dear—you needn't rub it in . . .

(*During the next speech* FRED *moves* L *round the table, so that at the end of the speech he is behind Norah*)

FRED. But I admired you for it. Still do. You know me. I thought I didn't want to marry. The way girls had started knocking around—going with anybody anywhere —turning themselves into damaged goods—I used to say to myself, "Nothing doing for you, Fred". And then you turned up—just the opposite—the old-fashioned, good, quiet kind. And—well—here we are. (*He gives her a pat on the shoulder*)

(*He cannot see* NORAH'S *face, which suddenly looks frightened*)

(*Preparing to leave*) Well . . .

NORAH (*stopping him with her voice*) Fred!

FRED (*halted*) What is it?

NORAH. Supposing I *wasn't* really like that—supposing

you'd made a mistake, not about me as I am now but as I was then—would it make any difference?

FRED (*jocular*) And supposing I was a black man five foot high and four foot broad . . .

NORAH. No, that's silly, Fred . . .

FRED. So was your question. They always are—those questions that begin with "supposing". I'm not a little, fat, black man—and I didn't make any mistake about you—thank God! Well, I'll go and earn my glass of bitter. Just one. And I'll come straight back. (*He moves* R *to the door*)

NORAH (*as he goes*) Yes, dear.

FRED (*suddenly returning to her*) But I'll give you a kiss first. (*He bends over and kisses her*) Just to stop you doing any more of that "supposing" . . .

(FRED *exits* R. NORAH *reflects for a few moments, then, with a sort of smiling shrug, as if dismissing an unpleasant possibility, goes on with her work. After another moment we hear a sharp tapping, as if against the window* L. NORAH *looks up, puzzled and rather frightened. After hesitating a moment, as the tapping continues, she rises, goes to the window* L *and peers through the gap in the curtains*)

NORAH (*calling through the window; puzzled*) Who is it? What do you want?

(*We cannot hear the reply.* NORAH *is still puzzled*)

Oh—all right. But I don't see why you shouldn't have come to the front door.

(NORAH *goes out* L *and after a moment returns, followed by* EVIE, *an unpleasant, flash-looking woman about thirty. They move* C)

(*Not liking the look of her*) Well, perhaps now you'll explain . . .

EVIE (*cutting in ruthlessly*) Got a drink?

NORAH. Only some cider.

EVIE (*contemptuously*) Do I look as if I drank cider?

NORAH (*tartly*) No, you don't. But I can't see that it

matters to me what you drink. Who are you? What do you want?

EVIE. You *are* Mrs Grant, aren't you?

NORAH. I told you at the door—yes, I am. But who are you?

EVIE (*with a grin*) I'm Evie—your daughter-in-law . . .

NORAH (*aghast*) I don't believe it.

EVIE. Then why the hell do you think I'm here?

NORAH. That's what I want to know.

EVIE (*with a flash of temper*) And I'm telling you. Look—I haven't time to do a variety act. I'm in a hurry. You've a son who goes by the name of Roy Flower—haven't you?

NORAH (*trying to brave it out*) No—I haven't. I've just told you—my name's Grant.

EVIE (*disgusted*) I know. Don't give me the run-around. Before your name was Grant, you had a son . . . (*She opens her bag to produce a snapshot*) He calls himself Roy Flower now, though I dare say he's had other names. Look—here he is——

(EVIE *shows the snapshot, which* NORAH *obviously recognizes*)

—and don't deny it—you're only wasting valuable time. He's told me all about it or I wouldn't be here, would I? He's your son, isn't he?

NORAH (*reluctantly*) Well, what if he is?

EVIE. I'm his wife . . .

NORAH. I don't believe it.

EVIE (*disgusted*) Oh—for God's sake! What have I to do—show you my marriage lines? As a matter of fact it doesn't matter whether we're married or I'm just living with him or we're only working together . . .

NORAH (*bitterly*) Working at what?

EVIE. Never mind what. But that brings me to the point. It never was healthy—and now they've tumbled to us—we'll be on the run any minute. That's why I came round to the back. They might be following me.

NORAH. Who might—the police?

EVIE (*with savage irony*) No—the Salvation Army. Look—have you got to be so dumb?

NORAH (*with spirit*) I wish you'd stop talking like somebody in a gangster film. You must have seen too many.

EVIE. If you want to know, I don't like 'em. Give me a good musical. But I didn't come here to talk about films . . .

NORAH (*sharply*) I don't see why you came here at all. Or why I should believe a word you say.

EVIE. Don't you? Well, just think a minute. How could I have known you had a son—if he didn't tell me? How many other people know? Even your husband doesn't know. Roy told me. That's proof enough, isn't it? (*Seeing the stricken look on* NORAH's *face*) Taken the starch out of you, hasn't it?

NORAH (*subdued*) Well—what do you want?

EVIE. You've got to help us. As I told you, we may be on the run any minute. We need money to get away. You'll have to cough up.

NORAH. Why should I? If you know my son as well as all that, you also ought to know that I told him some time ago I couldn't do anything more for him. I've helped him and helped him until I can't do any more. I warned him a dozen times . . .

EVIE (*cutting in*) Yes, but this is different. He's really in bad now . . .

NORAH. I've only your word for it . . .

EVIE. Then why should I take the chance of coming here?

NORAH. To get some more money out of me. He's tried and failed. So now you think you'll have a try. An easy trick.

EVIE. But I couldn't have come here unless he'd sent me.

NORAH. Of course you could. He could have told you about me—and then you could have decided to come here on your own . . .

EVIE. I didn't though. **As a matter** of fact he brought me here . . .

NORAH. Well, where is he?
EVIE. Not far away, but keeping out of sight. He thought it 'ud be safer for everybody if I came. After all, we're together. And, I tell you, very soon we might have to get out of town quick. And we're broke. So what about it?
NORAH. I'm not giving you anything.
EVIE. Your own son!
NORAH. He's had more than I can afford to give him already—and now I've only your word for it that he's in any danger . . .
EVIE. Well, he is—and so are you.
NORAH. Rubbish!
EVIE. Don't kid yourself. I know all about it. He told me. He's illegitimate. You had him brought up in the country, then when he ran away and finally got hold of you, you made him promise not to say anything because you never told your husband about him. You're frightened to death your husband'll get to know. And if you ask me, you were a dam' fool not to have told him right at the start . . .
NORAH. I'm not asking you—but I happen to agree with you. I *was* a fool not to have told him—and I've regretted it ever since . . .
EVIE (*triumphantly*) You daren't do it now—and what's going to happen if all this comes out?

(*There is a loud ring at the front door off* R. *It transforms* EVIE *into a quick whispering conspirator*)

Now listen—I'm going to fetch him and bring him round to the back. But we won't come in unless you've opened those curtains—(*she indicates the window* L) to show us it's safe to come in . . .

(*There is another ring at the front door*)

O.K.?
NORAH (*hastily*) All right.

(EVIE *hurries out* L *while* NORAH *exits* R *to the front door*)

HAMMOND (*off* R) Good evening, madam. I'm a police officer. I'd like a few words with you.
NORAH (*off* R) Very well. You'd better come in.
HAMMOND (*off* R) Thank you.

(NORAH *enters, followed by* HAMMOND, *a robust, middle-aged man in ordinary clothes, who looks round searchingly as he comes in*)

May I ask your name, madam?
NORAH. I'm Mrs Grant.
HAMMOND. Thank you. I'm Detective Inspector Hammond—(*putting a hand in his pocket*) if you'd like to see my warrant card . . .
NORAH (*smiling a little*) No, that isn't necessary, Inspector. I'm sure you're a genuine police inspector. Won't you sit down?

(NORAH *moves to the easy chair* L *and sits.* HAMMOND *moves to the easy chair* R *and sits*)

HAMMOND. Can I take it that the young woman who came into this house a few minutes ago has gone now?
NORAH. I think you can. I certainly hope she has.
HAMMOND. And why might that be, Mrs Grant?
NORAH (*with a slight smile*) Because, Inspector, I didn't like her.
HAMMOND. Not a friend of yours, then?
NORAH. Certainly not. I'd never set eyes on her before.
HAMMOND. What was she doing here then?
NORAH. Isn't it about time *I* asked a question? And before I ask it I'll tell you quite frankly I didn't know that young woman, never asked her to call here, and can't tell you what she does or where she lives. Now tell me something. Why are *you* interested in her?
HAMMOND. I'll be perfectly frank with you, Mrs Grant. That woman has had several names in her time, but she's generally known as Evie Pell. She's been inside —in prison—twice, and she's heading for it again. She's a thoroughly bad lot, Mrs Grant. Some of the people we have to go after, we're sorry for—it's more their misfor-

tune than their fault. But not somebody like Evie. She goes wrong out of choice. She's quite clever enough to make a living honestly if she wanted to. But she prefers being a crook. Not only that, but she's the type that often makes crooks out of fellows trying to go straight—uses her sex appeal—and so forth. A thoroughly bad lot—and, of course, we have her under observation, otherwise I wouldn't be here. Now you've got the picture of her, I hope, Mrs Grant?

NORAH. Yes. And none of it surprises me.

HAMMOND. Quite so. And now you'd better tell me what a woman of that sort was doing here, calling on you.

NORAH (*hesitatingly*) I'm in a very difficult position, Inspector.

HAMMOND (*cheerfully*) You'd be surprised how often I hear that.

NORAH. Possibly—but I can't believe there are many women in my position. I hope not—for their sakes. (*She hesitates*)

HAMMOND (*noticing the hesitation; gently*) I haven't too much time, Mrs Grant.

NORAH (*alarmed*) Neither have I. I'm glad you reminded me. Inspector, can I trust you . . . ?

HAMMOND. Mrs Grant, I can't pretend to promise that everything you tell me will be a dead secret between us. I just couldn't do that. But I can assure you that we're not interested in your private life, that if you confide in me I'll do my best to see that you're protected, and that the very best thing for you to do now is not to try and hide anything.

NORAH. I'm sure you're right. Very well. (*She hesitates, then takes the plunge*) When I was a girl I was in love with a man who made certain promises he didn't keep. I had an illegitimate child—a son. I was a secretary in the City and had a good job I didn't want to lose. So he was brought up in the country, though of course I often saw him. I thought I'd done with men—but about ten years ago a man I very much respected fell in love with me—and finally we got married. He—of course—is the Mr

Grant who lives here. (*She gives a faint smile*) Fortunately he decided to go out and have a glass of bitter. Otherwise, I couldn't be telling you all this.

HAMMOND. Because you never told him?

NORAH. I never told him. He's a very kind man but rather strict and narrow in some ways. I couldn't bring myself to tell him. It was foolish. It was wrong. I know that now—and—(*with some signs of distress*) and I've paid for it over and over again. It's always been a kind of shadow between us—though I don't think he ever guesses anything. We'd have been perfectly happy if I hadn't had this secret. If only I could have told him about Roy—my son—but of course once I'd decided to say nothing, that was impossible. The longer I kept it quiet, the harder it would have been to say anything, the greater the shock would have been to him. And what made it much worse was that Roy became such a trouble to me—never settling down—always having to be helped...

HAMMOND. He knew? Your son, I mean.

NORAH (*distressed*) Yes, I felt I had to tell him—and he didn't take it very well—and began to blame me for all his misfortunes—and then, of course, I began to blame myself...

HAMMOND. Don't you do that, Mrs Grant, if you've tried to do your best for him—as I'm sure you have. He's in his twenties now, I take it? Well, it's time he stood on his own feet. Now tell me about Evie.

NORAH. She told me she was married to him. Do you think that's true?

HAMMOND (*grimly*) No—but of course she might be living with him...

NORAH. She said they might have to leave London—and they hadn't any money...

HAMMOND. That part might be true.

NORAH. She wanted money from me, of course...

HAMMOND. Did you give her any?

NORAH. No. I pointed out that I'd only her word for it... (*She hesitates*)

HAMMOND. And then what?

NORAH. We heard you ringing the front door bell—and she hurried out at the back . . . (*She stops*)

(HAMMOND *looks at her enquiringly, and she returns his look rather blankly*)

HAMMOND (*who is suspicious*) Is that all?
NORAH (*braving it out*) Yes, Inspector.
HAMMOND (*gravely*) I don't think so, Mrs Grant.
NORAH (*trying to carry it off*) Really—Inspector—are you suggesting I'm deliberately deceiving you?
HAMMOND (*steadily*) Yes, I am.
NORAH (*rising, still trying to brave it*) Then I think there's nothing more to be said . . .
HAMMOND (*rising*) No, no, no, Mrs Grant. That won't do at all. You're in too far to retreat like that. I know very well you're keeping something from me. To begin with, I'm certa n a woman like Evie wouldn't have run off without trying to fix something. And then again, you gave yourself away. By your change of manner. I'm an old hand, Mrs Grant. I've spent thousands of hours questioning people. And whenever a woman suddenly looks blank, as you did, and then goes all dignified and haughty on me, I know very well she's stopped telling me the truth. I'm willing to bet all the money in my pocket that Evie suggested some arrangement before she left. Come now.
NORAH. You're right, of course. (*She moves restlessly down* L, *clearly not knowing what to do*)
HAMMOND (*warning her*) Time's precious. Come on, Mrs Grant. Tell me the truth.
NORAH (*distressed*) But it's my own son, Inspector. How can I?
HAMMOND. Now listen to me carefully. Did you know he'd—gone wrong?
NORAH. No. I sometimes suspected he might. I know he's weak—foolish . . .
HAMMOND. That's what I guessed. Now, believe me, the worst thing that can happen to this lad is that he gets away with somebody like Evie. After that he won't have a chance to go straight. He'll be in it up to the neck,

A GLASS OF BITTER

she'll see to that. His only chance is to be picked up now, before he's gone too far. The worst that can happen to him is better than the best that could happen to him on the run with Evie. Help him to get away now and you make a criminal out of him, Mrs Grant.

NORAH (*distressed*) I dare say you're right—but do you realize what you're asking me to do?

HAMMOND. I'd ask my own wife to do it in the same circumstances . . .

NORAH. I might never forgive myself . . .

HAMMOND. You may never forgive yourself if you don't co-operate with us . . .

NORAH (*much distressed*) I don't know what to do . . .

HAMMOND. There's only one thing to do—for his sake as well as yours and ours. Come now, Mrs Grant.

NORAH (*moving* C; *arriving at a decision*) I've got to convince myself, Inspector. You must allow me to do that. I have to live with myself—and I'm a woman, a mother. Please let me convince myself that you're right. Isn't there some signal I could give you—if I see plainly you *are* right?

HAMMOND. If you want it that way—yes. Open those curtains . . . (*He points to the curtains on the window* R)

(NORAH *gives a mirthless little laugh*)

What's the matter? Done that before?

NORAH. No, but I seem to have heard of it.

HAMMOND (*preparing to go*) I'll be outside there, waiting. I'll leave the front door off the latch so that I can come straight in. And remember, Mrs Grant, I'm doing this purely for your sake. It's no longer necessary from my point of view because I've a good idea what's going to happen. But I want you to satisfy yourself and feel all right about this. The curtains then.

(HAMMOND *exits quickly* R. NORAH *takes a compact from her handbag, looks at herself in it, does a little quick powdering, etc., and then goes to the window* L *and pulls back the curtains. Then she moves* C *and waits, obviously getting herself under control*

After a moment or two EVIE *and* ROY *enter* L, *rather cautiously. He is a rather shabbily dressed youth, and clearly a weak character. He wears an old raincoat.* EVIE *moves to* L *of the easy chair* L *and* ROY *stands just* R *of the doorway*)

ROY. I'm here, you see, Mother.
NORAH. Yes.
ROY. It would have saved a lot of time and trouble if you'd believed what Evie told you.
EVIE. Who *was* that who called?
NORAH. Just a friend.
EVIE (*suspiciously*) Gone, I hope?
NORAH. Yes.
EVIE (*to Roy*) Well, go on, tell her yourself.
ROY. It looks like we're in trouble, Mother. We'll have to get out of town—sharp. We need some money—you'll have to help us.
NORAH. Why should I? I told you last time you couldn't expect any more help from me.
ROY. This is different.
NORAH. Why is it different?

(ROY *hesitates*)

EVIE. Go on—tell her. She wouldn't believe me.
ROY. We got mixed up in something that didn't come off quite right. So now the police are on to us. We've got to get away.
EVIE (*grimly*) No kidding!
NORAH. She might have to get away—but why should you?
EVIE (*disgusted*) Oh—for God's sake!
ROY. Because I'm in it just as much as she is.
NORAH. All right, suppose you are? Suppose they arrest you?
ROY (*indignantly*) What are you talking like that for? *Suppose they arrest me!* Then I'm for it, aren't I? Do you want to see me in the dock—then sent to prison? You're my mother, aren't you?
EVIE. Yes—and *your* little story isn't going to look too good when it comes out, is it?

Roy (*almost hysterically*) I tell you, I've got to get away. What's the matter with you?

Evie. She still doesn't believe us, Roy. She still thinks it's a gag to get a few more quid out of her.

Roy (*desperate*) Look—this isn't a gag. I tell you—I might be on the run by tomorrow morning—they may be looking for me tonight, for all I know. Don't stand there looking as if I was trying to touch you for a pound or two to take me to the Dogs. This is *serious*. I got mixed up in a big warehouse job—worth thousands if it had come off—but it came unstuck—and one fellow I was working with got picked up. *Now* do you understand, stupid!

Norah. I'm not stupid and I quite understand, Roy. You've stopped trying to earn an honest living—you never tried very hard—and now this woman is turning you into a thief. You've bungled something, which doesn't surprise me, and now you're in danger of being arrested.

Evie (*sneering*) She's got it at last!

Norah. Now suppose I do give you some money, what will you do?

Evie. What do you think? Buy some pretty ornaments?

Norah (*losing her temper*) Oh—you be quiet. I'm talking to him.

Evie (*savagely*) If you ask me, you're talking to yourself. He wants the money so that he can get away, go somewhere where they aren't looking for him. We've told you twenty times.

Roy. Evie and I thought we'd make for Liverpool. She has some friends there.

Norah. What sort of friends?

Roy (*angrily*) What does that matter, so long as they can keep us under cover for a bit?

Norah. And then—what?

Roy (*impatiently*) Then when things are quieter we'll come back to London.

Norah. And try to break into another warehouse. Or will it be a house next time?

Evie (*disgusted*) No—Buckingham Palace.

NORAH (*ignoring her; to Roy*) Can't you see what I'm getting at? If I help you to get away, all I'm doing is helping to make a criminal out of you. You're probably only half in it now. In a month or two you'll be in it for the rest of your life.

EVIE. Keep her there, Roy.

ROY. Why—what's the idea?

EVIE. I'm going to look through those tins on the kitchen shelf. Lots of women keep housekeeping money in one of those tins. So keep her here.

(EVIE *exits* L)

NORAH. I'm not going to put up with that . . .

(NORAH *tries to follow Evie, but* ROY *blocks her way*)

ROY (*sulkily*) She's desperate. It's your own fault. Come on, be sensible.

NORAH (*distressed*) But can't you see, Roy, that your only chance now is to face whatever the police want to charge you with, to get it over and done with, to take the consequences of what you've done—then make a clean fresh start?

ROY. At what?

NORAH. I don't know . . .

ROY. Neither do I. What a hope I've had . . .

NORAH. You talked like that to me before—and I used to believe you. Now I don't. I don't believe you've ever really tried. It would have been better for both of us if I'd refused to help you two or three years ago. Then you might have tried to make a real man out of yourself. But you're not going to turn yourself into a regular criminal with my help.

ROY (*indignantly*) Call yourself a mother!

NORAH. Yes, because I'm thinking what's best for you. (*Imploring*) Roy—please—for your own sake—go to the police—give yourself up. It'll make it all the better for you.

ROY. No bloody fear! What do you take me for? Give myself up! Talk sense.

NORAH. It's your only chance, Roy.

Roy. My only chance is for you to give me ten quid—or five'll do at a pinch—and then for Evie and me to clear out tonight. And if you won't give me the money, I'll take it, that's all.

(EVIE *enters* L)

EVIE. Not from that kitchen, you won't, sonny boy. Nothing there. Must be here somewhere. (*Looking round*) Where's her bag?

NORAH (*indignantly; about to move*) Don't you touch my bag . . .

EVIE (*still looking*) Keep her away, Roy.

(ROY *blocks Norah's way*)

NORAH (*in despair*) Oh—very well. (*She crosses to the window* R *and pulls back the curtains*)

EVIE (*in alarm*) Here—what's she up to? Draw those curtains again, Roy.

(ROY *crosses to the window* R *and draws the curtains.* EVIE *finds Norah's bag on the easy chair* L)

(*Triumphantly*) It's here. I've got it. (*She begins to ransack the bag*)

NORAH (*moving* C; *in despair*) Oh—you fool . . .

ROY (*sulkily*) Serves you right. We've got to have it. How much is there?

EVIE (*finding some bank-notes in the bag*) Seven quid. It'll do nicely.

(HAMMOND *enters* R)

HAMMOND. So it will, Evie. But put it down, I might want it as evidence.

(EVIE *puts down the bag on the table*)

ROY (*alarmed*) Who are you?

EVIE (*moving* L; *shouting*) He's a rozzer.

(EVIE *exits* L. HAMMOND *moves to* ROY *and puts a hand on his arm, though* ROY *is really too dazed to do anything.* NORAH, *distressed, collapses into the easy chair* L)

HAMMOND. Don't try anything, lad. You might get hurt. You're coming with me to answer a few questions about the East India Warehouse job . . .

ROY (*sulkily*) I don't know anything about it.

HAMMOND. Ever heard of "shopping"? It means spilling the beans, mentioning some names. They're not supposed to do it, but they do it all the time. You don't understand yet the company you've been keeping. For instance, there's Evie, who's just left us in such a hurry . . .

ROY. Well, you haven't got her, have you?

HAMMOND. Don't be silly. Of course we have. I'd two good men outside that back door. But of course she didn't know that. Evie was clearing out—and never mind what happened to you. She got you into the mess, but she wasn't staying to try to get you out of it. That's Evie. And then—take Quinn. You've never heard of him, have you?

ROY. No.

HAMMOND. I wouldn't stick to that, if I were you. We can prove you knew him fairly well. But you didn't know him well enough. I'll tell you two things about friend Quinn. First, he's Evie's steady man, so far as she has one. She was just kidding you. The other thing is that it was Quinn we picked up on this warehouse job—and he's the one that shopped you. Not nice, is it? But then, you see, these aren't a nice class of people. The only thing for you to do is to forget about 'em—make up your mind, when we're finished with you, never to have anything to do with 'em ever again.

NORAH (*distressed*) Oh—Roy—I had to do it—for your own sake . . .

HAMMOND. Quite right, Mrs Grant. (*He crosses* L *to the door and goes just off stage. Calling*) O.K., Ferguson? I'm sending the other one out. Take 'em both in—I'll be along soon. Go easy with the boy—he's new to it. (*He pops back and beckons to Roy*) Come on, lad. They're waiting for you. And don't look at your mother like that. Later on, you'll understand it's the best thing that could have happened to you.

(NORAH *begins to cry quietly*)

ROY (*crossing* L *to the door; sulkily*) Go to hell!
HAMMOND (*cheerfully*) No need. I work there. Now go on—and mind your manners with the sergeants—they aren't as patient as I am.

(ROY *exits* L. HAMMOND *looks at Norah and moves towards her*)

You're upset, Mrs Grant. It's natural. But don't take it to heart. You couldn't have done a better thing—for his sake. There's many a good man started off on the wrong foot like that—put himself right and laughed at the silly ideas he used to have. The lad'll be all right. I'll put in a quiet word for him—and we're easy on first offenders these days . . .
NORAH (*muffled*) Yes, I know. It's not that. It's having —to—give away my own son—as I did . . .
HAMMOND. A glass of bitter doesn't last long, you know.
NORAH (*remembering, looking up now*) Oh . . .
HAMMOND. Might be back any minute. You wouldn't like him to see you like this, would you?
NORAH (*getting up*) No. Will you excuse me? I'll go up to my bedroom. (*She sees her bag and remembers*) Oh—will you really want that money as evidence?
HAMMOND (*smiling*) No—I just said that to give Evie a jolt. We've plenty against her without bringing in either you or your bag.
NORAH (*taking her bag*) Thank you, Inspector.

(NORAH *exits quickly* R. HAMMOND *waits a moment, looks round to see if everything looks all right, moves to the door* L, *looks off stage for a moment, then moves* LC *and lights a pipe or cigarette.*

After a moment, FRED GRANT *enters* R. *He and* HAMMOND *look at each other for a moment, without expression. This suspense should be held as long as possible. Then they close in* C *and talk very quietly*)

FRED. All right, Inspector?

HAMMOND. Yes, Mr Grant. Just like I said it would be.
FRED. He came here?
HAMMOND. My chaps have just taken him down to the station. When Mrs Grant gave me the signal, he and the woman were just about to take the money out of her bag.
FRED. But she gave you the signal?
HAMMOND. Yes. She saw for herself. That was the best way.
FRED. Is she taking it badly?
HAMMOND. Upset, naturally. Any woman would be. But having to pretend with you will do her good.
FRED. So you think I oughtn't to tell her?
HAMMOND. Yes, I do. Never let on. Much better now.
FRED. What'll happen to the boy?
HAMMOND. Nothing serious. Enough to do him good. And—let's hope—keep him away from the wide boys in future. To say nothing of the wide girls, who are even worse. (*Moving towards Fred and lowering his voice even more*) Tell me, Mr Grant, how did you get on to the boy in the the first place?
FRED. I'd guessed for a long time there was something wrong. By her manner. She was spending too much as well. I began putting two and two together—then one evening I followed her—and after that I had some enquiries made. (*He pauses*) I hope she won't be dragged into this business.
HAMMOND. No reason why she should. Well—you haven't seen me. Good night, Mr Grant, I'll go this way.

(HAMMOND *exits* L. FRED *moves to the easy chair* R, *settles down in it and begins taking another look at the evening paper.*
After a moment or two NORAH *comes in* R, *looking quite composed now. She moves towards the easy chair* L)

NORAH. Oh—you're back, Fred.
FRED. Just had one glass, as I said I would, and gave the local darts team a cheer. They're playing a match tonight—great excitement!
NORAH (*sitting in the easy chair* L *and smiling at him*) I

believe I can still see signs of it. Did you get worked up? (*She picks up her mending from the work-basket*)

FRED. Just a little perhaps. You know, Norah, a lot can happen while you're drinking a glass of bitter.

NORAH. I'm sure it can, Fred.

> NORAH *continues with her darning and* FRED *reads the paper, exactly as they were at the beginning of the play, as—*

the CURTAIN *slowly falls*

FURNITURE AND PROPERTY PLOT

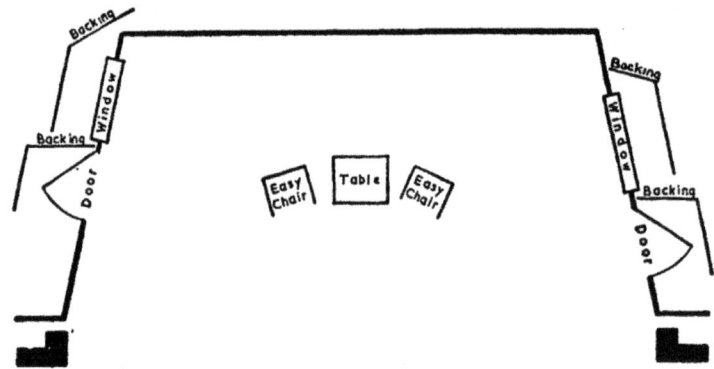

On stage: Small table
    Easy chair (R). *On it:* evening newspaper
    Easy chair (L). *On it:* Norah's handbag with banknotes and compact
        Beside it: work-basket with mending, etc.

Personal: EVIE: handbag with snapshot
    HAMMOND: pipe (or cigarettes), matches
    FRED: pipe, tobacco

LIGHTING PLOT

Property fittings required: centre light or standard lamp

Interior

A sitting-room. Evening
    THE MAIN ACTING AREAS are round the easy chair (L), the easy chair (R), the door (R), the door (L)
    THE APPARENT SOURCE OF LIGHT is from those practical lamps used
    OFF STAGE LIGHTING: strips outside doors, darkness outside both windows

To open: warm, artificial lighting

No cues